Subconscious Mind

Tame, Reprogram & Control Your Subconscious Mind To Transform Your Life

Your Free Gift

As a way of thanking you for the purchase, I'd like to offer you a complimentary gift:

- **5 Pillar Life Transformation Checklist:** This short book is about life transformation, presented in bit size pieces for easy implementation. I believe that without such a checklist, you are likely to have a hard time implementing anything in this book and any other thing you set out to do religiously and sticking to it for the long haul. It doesn't matter whether your goals relate to weight loss, relationships, personal finance, investing, personal development, improving communication in your family, your overall health, finances, improving your sex life, resolving issues in your relationship, fighting PMS successfully, investing, running a successful business, traveling etc. With a checklist like this one, you can bet that anything you do will seem a lot easier to implement until the end. Therefore, even if you don't continue reading this book, at least read the one thing that will help you in every other aspect of your life. Grab your copy now by clicking/tapping here or simply enter http://bit.ly/2fantonfreebie into your browser. Your life will never be the same again (if you implement what's in this book), I promise.

PS: I'd like your feedback. If you are happy with this book, please leave a review on Amazon.

Introduction

Your subconscious mind can be your greatest ally or greatest foe. Whether it hinders or helps you live a great life is entirely up to how you program it and above that, how you use it to propel yourself away from things you do not want and towards those that you want.

At the most basic level, your subconscious mind is in charge of your automatic thoughts and behaviors. Since a large percentage of your life is a reflection of your habits and most common thoughts, when you exercise control over your subconscious mind, it becomes easier to ensure that your habits and thoughts are good and therefore, you are living a life that aligns with your highest desires.

On the other hand, when you let your subconscious mind operate with no semblance of conscious control of what it concentrates on and makes habitual, the probability of your life being desirable (to you and others) is slim.

To live a great life, a life where you are not only enthusiastic but also capable of making the habitual changes that drive you towards progress, prosperity, abundance, and whatever else you desire in your life, you need to learn how to control, reprogram, and make your subconscious mind your b*tch. This book is going to show you how to do that.

I hope you enjoy it!

Table of Contents

Your Free Gift _____ 2

Introduction _____ 3

Meet Your Subconscious Mind, Your Most Powerful Ally _____ 7

   Understanding How the Subconscious Mind Works With the Other Levels of the Mind _____ 10

The Benefits Of Controlling Your Subconscious Mind _____ 17

   The Advantages of Controlling and Reprograming your Subconscious _____ 17

How To Control Your Subconscious Mind And Make It Your Bitch _____ 23

Rules Of Reprogramming Your Subconscious Mind _____ 33

   How To Reprogram Your Subconscious _____ 34

Bonus! Additional Ways To Communicate With, And Reprogram Your Subconscious Mind _____ 39

Conclusion _____ 42

Do You Like My Book & Approach To Publishing? _____ 43

1: First, I'd Love It If You Leave a Review of This Book on Amazon. _____ *43*

2: Check Out My Emotional Mastery Books ___ *43*

3: Grab Some Freebies On Your Way Out; Giving Is Receiving, Right? _____ *44*

PSS: Let Me Also Help You Save Some Money! _____ 45

Subconscious Mind

© Copyright 2018 by Fantonpublishers.com - All rights reserved.

Meet Your Subconscious Mind, Your Most Powerful Ally

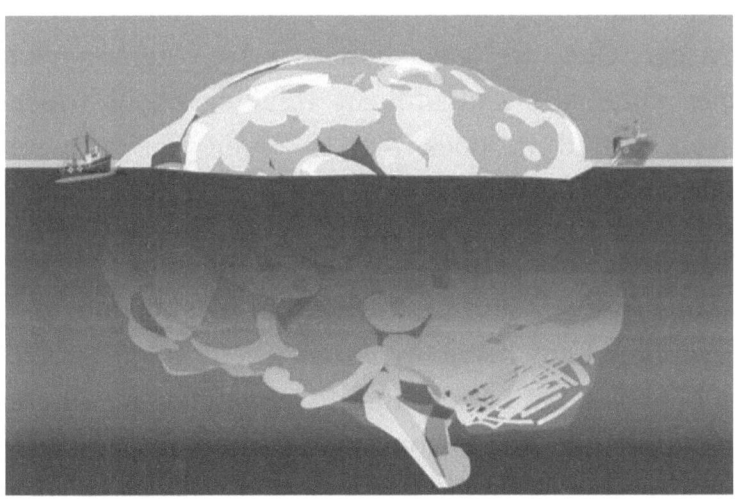

Between the years 1856-1939, Sigmund Freud, an Austrian psychologist, hypothesized that our brains have a 3 level mind model that divides the mind into three levels as follows:

1. **The Conscious mind:** This level of the mind is responsible for all conscious thoughts and actions, the thoughts and actions presently in your awareness. For instance, when you are concentrating on mastery of a new move or completion of an important work project, you are using the conscious mind in the same way you use it to smell the fragrance of a rose and take in its beauty.

2. **The Subconscious mind:** This level is subliminal and therefore in control of the more automatic aspects of our lives such as breathing and specific thoughts and actions.

Although most of the reactions controlled by this level of the brain are automatic, thinking about them engages the conscious mind. A great example of this is our ability to drive a car. Once we learn how to drive, the behavior becomes automatic and only by thinking about which gear you shifted to does driving enter your present awareness (the conscious mind).

3. **The unconscious mind:** This level of the mind is home to all our memories and past events. In most instances—the exception here being hypnosis where some people under hypnosis have been able to remember details of their younger life—the unconscious mind is inaccessible. A great example of this is the first step we took or at a deeper level, how it felt to say our first word(s).

While most of us are aware of the existence of the subconscious mind, very few of us are aware of what it is, how it operates, or how to activate, command, and reprogram it. Before we discuss how to activate and reprogram the subconscious mind, we need to understand how the three levels of the mind work together and why the subconscious mind can be such a powerful ally or foe if used correctly or incorrectly respectively.

Subconscious Mind

Understanding How the Subconscious Mind Works With the Other Levels of the Mind

Think of your mind as a triangle.

At the very top is the conscious mind, the most accessible part of the brain. This level of the brain/mind takes up a very small portion of your brain capacity (some researchers have pegged its capacity at 10%). Below it is the subconscious mind.

The subconscious or preconscious takes a larger portion of the triangle with some hypothesizing that it makes up 50-60 or your overall brainpower. Below the subconscious is the unconscious mind that occupies the base of the triangle and makes up 30-40% of your overall brainpower of capacity. Because of how deep and vast it is, much like the floor of the ocean, it is inaccessible to the conscious mind and to communicate with it—mostly to retrieve memories—the conscious mind has to go through the subconscious mind.

How the three levels of the brain work together and individually is very intricate.

In the most basic of terms, your conscious mind is where you live most of your conscious life; it acts as a commander giving out orders to the subconscious and unconscious mind. Although the conscious mind is the captain, its role stops at giving orders. The subconscious and unconscious levels of the mind are responsible for executing the orders in accordance to their training (learned behavior and habits).

Your conscious mind is responsible for your communication with the outside world and your inner self through self-talk, visual images, thought, and overall actions. On its part, the subconscious is responsible for communication between the conscious and the unconscious mind as well as your recent memories and habits.

In addition to being the storehouse for all your memories and experiences, the unconscious mind, in communication with the conscious and subconscious mind, also uses these memories—even those consciously forgotten—to mold your habits, behaviors, and beliefs about yourself, others, and life in general.

Subconscious Mind

The constant interaction between the unconscious and conscious mind aided by the subconscious mind is what adds meaning to life. It is also through this three-way communication that we filter the world, use our imagination, express our feelings and sensation, and dream.

If you may, conceptualize your mind as a computer:

In such a case, the monitor and keyword would be the conscious mind because the conscious mind is the avenue through which we filter and input information into the mind with external stimuli being the keyboard and your conscious awareness being the monitor upon which inputted data displays.

In this scenario, your subconscious mind is like the ram in your computer, the module where currently in use programs and data reside so that should you need them instantly, they are available. The subconscious mind (ram) is home to your recent memories and the programs you run most such as habits, behaviors, recurring thoughts, and feelings.

Your unconscious mind is like the hard drive upon which you store data long-term as well as default programs (those learnt and instilled since birth). Together with the subconscious mind, your unconscious mind uses these programs to make sense of everything in your environment with its ultimate goal being to ensure your survival.

Subconscious Mind

This explanation of how the three minds work together is very important because, since your mind is like a computer that learns from your environment (input), if you are not consciously aware of the information you are feeding your "computer," the results will be a formation of a warped worldview.

Think of it this way.

Your conscious mind controls your ability to focus and imagine what is not yet real to you. Because the conscious mind is the captain of the ship, what it chooses to focus on and imagine passes on to the subconscious and unconscious minds. The subconscious filters this information to determine how important it is to you and if the input is important, it keeps it ready for access and passes the information on to the unconscious mind that, by creating memories of the instance, establishes a pattern of some sort.

Compared to your conscious mind, your subconscious has a stronger sense of awareness (we often refer to this as sixth sense), which is why because it is always on, it is a slave to your conscious mind.

If the thoughts most constant in your conscious mind are negative, your subconscious and, to some degree, unconscious mind will reflect this and deliver to you all the negative memories, emotions, feelings, and habits (this is one of the reason why mastering your subconscious mind through affirmation is so important) associated to what is in your present awareness.

Moreover, because your subconscious mind knows no difference between reality and make belief, the negative thoughts, memories, habits, and experiences will seep into your reality. As you can imagine, when this happens, your life becomes a hard-to-escape negativity that leads to phobias, stress, anxiety, failures, and every bad situation you can imagine.

Your ability to focus and direct your conscious attention/awareness is what gives you the ability to reprogram your subconscious mind and the very thing you need to utilize to make your subconscious mind your bitch.

Fortunately, directing your conscious awareness is not rocket science. All you have to do is make a conscious decision to be in control of the thoughts you allow into your conscious awareness. Obviously, mastery of this requires a ton of practice and patience. Later on in the guide, we shall discuss specific strategies you can use to take control of your conscious awareness, the things presently in your focus.

Subconscious Mind

The conscious mind uses words (thoughts) to pass commands to the subconscious mind. It is also capable of using imagination/visualization: your mind has the ability to imagine things hitherto unheard off or seen. Because the subconscious mind lacks the ability to distinguish reality from anything imagined by the conscious mind, you can also use creative visualization to reprogram your subconscious mind.

For instance, if, to experience happiness, by intently visualizing being in a place that offers you comfort and all the happiness you could ever need, your happy place, you can actually get the subconscious mind to call up all the feelings, emotions, and habits associated with the visualization.

Subconscious Mind

Now that you understand how the subconscious mind works in tandem with the other levels of the mind, let us discuss the benefits of controlling your subconscious mind.

The Benefits Of Controlling Your Subconscious Mind

The most amazing thing about your subconscious mind is that it never gets tired, which is why it works all the time—even when you are sleeping—and always obeys orders relayed by the conscious mind.

While the subconscious mind does indeed control a large swath of your processing power and your life, it cannot do so without direction from your conscious mind, which is why the subconscious and unconscious mind only delivers the feelings, emotions, habits, and behavior of that which takes up the most space in your conscious awareness.

Given what we have discussed thus far, here are the most standout benefits of gaining control over your subconscious mind:

The Advantages of Controlling and Reprograming your Subconscious

Before we start discussing the various benefits that come with making your subconscious mind your bitch, we have to mention that your subconscious mind is capable of processing upwards of 100 billion bits of information per second. In comparison, the conscious mind can only process 40 bits per second. This alone makes your subconscious mind immensely powerful.

While exerting control over the subconscious mind is no small task, if you patiently implement the processes we shall discuss in later sections of this guide, you will derive the following benefits:

Better Relationships

Of the many mental tasks handled by your subconscious mind, one is the ability to connect memories in your unconscious to present stimuli presently in your conscious awareness.

Working together, the three minds combine old memories to new one thus helping you determine how to manage specific relationships by determining things such as what to say when. When your mind can easily relate what you or someone else is feeling to something you have experienced before, it becomes easier to create a trusting connection. This alone has the ability to improve all your relationships.

As stated earlier, the subconscious mind is like a RAM that houses often-run programs. In conjunction with the unconscious mind, it helps store your past in story form and bundled together so that they are relatable and so that when you need to access them especially in relation to responses with a relationship partner, they are easy to access and relate to the necessary response for the relationship at hand.

It is because of the interplay between the three levels of your mind that you know when to be remorseful, witty, loving, friendly, geeky, and all the other personalize emotions that come with specific relations.

Untapped Power

In his book, The Genie Within your Subconscious Mind, Harry Carpenter calls the subconscious mind a genie that is willing to grant your every wish provided you know how to talk to it and ask for favors.

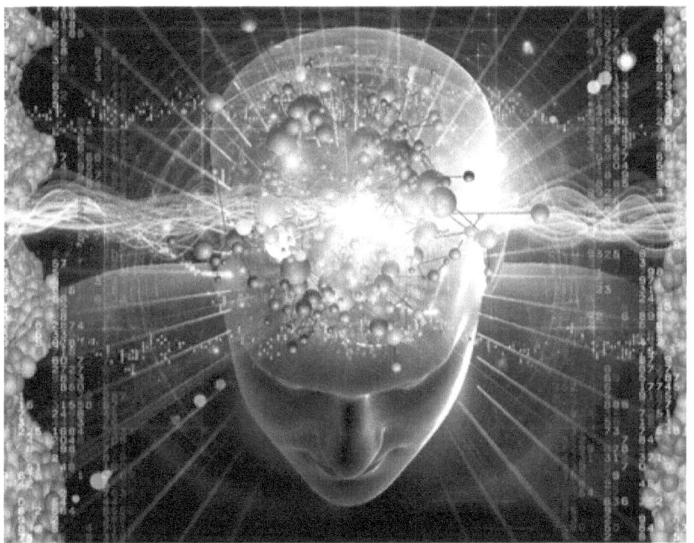

As illustrated by the computing power of the subconscious mind (it takes up 50-60% of your overall computing power), your subconscious is very powerful (100 billion bits of information in seconds is no joke). What does this translate to?

This translates into a well of untapped power that when you decide to tap, will change everything about your life including how you think and reason, how you (or your ability to) achieve your goals, how you relate with others, your level of satisfaction with your life, your success and happiness, and everything else touching every pillar of your life.

By reprogramming your mind, you can change any aspect of your personality. If you want to be more loving and less angry, visualizing yourself as a loving, less angry person and then using affirmative words to reinforce this state will make you a more loving and less angry person.

Likewise, if you want to adopt healthy habits one at a time, by consciously focusing on the habit you want to adopt, the conscious mind will transmit this information to the subconscious mind, which will then determine its importance and ask the unconscious mind to bring forth the memories attached to this.

Another aspect of subconscious mind is that we also call it the universal mind because of its innate connection with the universe. The programs most run by your subconscious mind influence your thoughts and behavioral patterns. When the programs are positive, your thoughts and emotions will be positive meaning, thanks to the law of attraction, you will attract into your life similar emotions and experiences.

Subconscious Mind

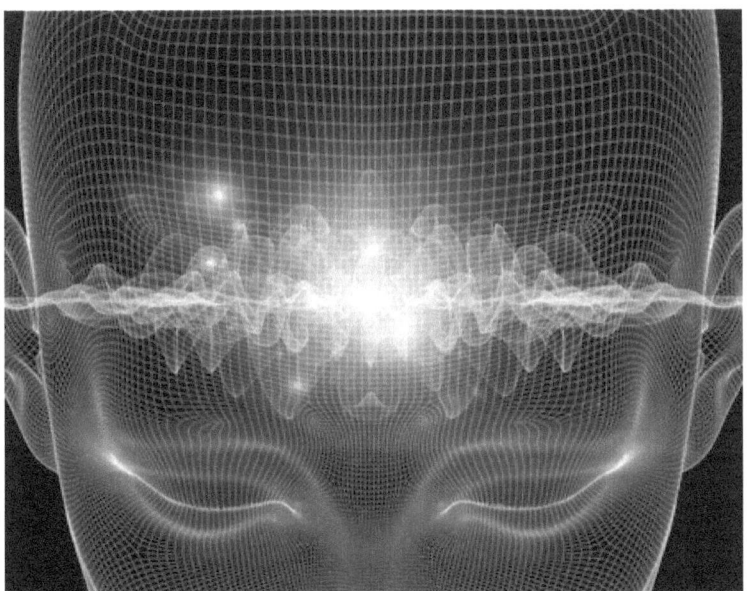

The power of the subconscious is unrivaled and therefore, the benefits of making your subconscious mind your slave are many. Included in this repertoire of benefits is:

1. Better health and improved wellbeing

2. Improved creativity and problem solving abilities

3. Easier composure and relaxation

4. The ability to eliminate limiting belief and overcome the pain of trauma

5. Improved happiness and an innate sense of purpose and control

Subconscious Mind

These benefits, and the many we have not mentioned here should motivate you to control your subconscious mind, which the next section shows you how to do.

How To Control Your Subconscious Mind And Make It Your Bitch

At the heart of controlling your subconscious mind is this one thig: *the need to change your thought patterns.*

You must remember that your subconscious mind lacks reasoning capability, which is why it is a slave to the commands of the conscious mind. To control your subconscious mind thus making it your bitch (in the sense that it obeys every one of your commands), you need to take control of your consciousness.

The strategies you can use to control your mind are many; with that stated, below are the most effective ways to control your subconscious mind and make it your bitch.

1: Control your subjective thoughts

As we have stated many times, thoughts, especially those you give conscious awareness, are very powerful: they have the ability to manifest as physical things in your life.

Thoughts are not equal, which is why our thoughts can be objective and subjective. Objective thoughts are those bred from general reasoning or thinking; a great example here is thoughts bred from study or recollection. Often, such thoughts lack feeling and therefore cannot affect the subconscious mind or get it to release emotions or feelings of any sort.

Subconscious Mind

Subjective thoughts are thoughts existing in the mind and bred from thinking; they are not an "object of thought." When focused on and given enough emotional power, such thoughts have the ability to enter into and influence the subconscious mind. Worry is a great example of a subjective thought. The more you worry, the more anxious and worrisome you will get because the subconscious mind will be communicating with the unconscious and asking it to recall all the times you have worried and implement the habits/patterns you used to handle it.

To use subjective thoughts as a way to control your subconscious mind, use emotion-infused affirmations (positive self-talk). Saying something as simple as, "I am a radiant ray of happiness" and then visualizing yourself as being happy (infusing the affirmation with emotional power), will change the subconscious patterns associated with happiness, the ones in your RAM.

While still on subjective thoughts, you should note that controlling your conscious awareness is a choice, a decision. Make the decision to become aware of your conscious thoughts—especially as you engage in tasks that do not require active brainpower: bathing, brushing your teeth, washing the dishes, cooking etc.—and make the choice to or not admit specific thoughts.

Learning how to observe your conscious thoughts from moment to moment takes tons of practice. The best way to get started on this path is to practice mindfulness meditation. Mindfulness meditation is relatively easy to practice since we have many guided meditation and innovative meditation apps. This resource has some great meditation sessions and apps:

Although mindfulness meditation is essential, you do not explicitly need it because once you shift your focus to your internal state—the thoughts passing through your mind from moment to moment—you will have a level of control over your conscious thoughts and their responses.

When you notice negative thoughts, which you will primarily because the mind is negative-inclined—it notices negatives more than it notices positives—do not wish them away. Take a moment to observe the thought, accept its existence, and then let it fade out of your conscious awareness.

To keep negative thoughts from becoming subjective and emotion-laced—meaning they have the ability to affect your subconscious mind—question negative thoughts as they arise and then reword them into positive statements/affirmation. For instance, if a negative, worrisome thought says, "you shall lose your job," counter it with a positive thought such as, "I'm a valuable employee who contributes to the company growth. If I continue working diligently, I shall be up for a promotion in no time." Such a thought will whitewash over the emotional negativity brought on by the first thought. If you practice this every time you have this thought, you will rewire your subconscious mind into believing you have job security.

With subjective thoughts, repetition is key. The more you enforce positive thoughts, the higher the chances that your subconscious mind will recognize the positive thoughts as important, and the more likely that it shall bend to the will of your positive programing.

2: Use Substitution

Substitution (we have discussed it in passing) is an effective way to stop negative thoughts in their tracks. As the name of the technique suggests, the idea is to become aware of your moment to moment conscious thoughts so that when you notice a negative thought, you can replace it with a suitable (adjacent and countering) positive thought.

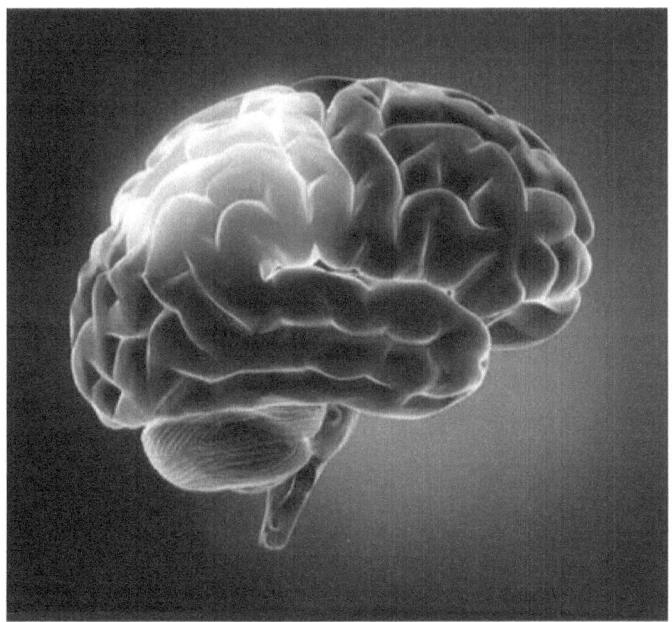

Through the power of substitution, a mind prone to negative thinking can easily become a mind prone to positive thinking. The ability to notice negative in time to substitute them with positive ones takes time to master especially for someone whose mind has grown accustomed to negative thought patterns.

To short-circuit a mind prone to negativity (remember that your most common thoughts leave trace programs in the subconscious mind and develop behavioral patterns in your unconscious mind), you also need to make a decision: a decision to start seeing the good in everything (develop what we call a positive mindset, which coincidentally, you can do through visualization and affirmation).

The ways by which you can get your conscious mind to stop concentrating on negativity and start concentrating on the positivity in everything are many. The most effective of these ways, given that making your subconscious mind pliable to your commands happens through the conscious mind, is journaling.

Maintain a gratitude journal (keep it with you at all times) and as you go about your day, constantly be on the lookout for things that fill you with gratitude. Now, assuming you are swimming in negativity, the thought of finding something to be grateful for may seem laughable; it is not.

When you are grateful, you are looking at the things you have instead of the things you do not have; this itself has immense power. For instance, instead of looking at your well-used computer, with dents and cracks all over, and thinking, "I wish I had the money to buy myself the latest MacBook Pro," make the conscious decision to think, "Wow! This laptop has served me well over the years. I appreciate all the work it has helped me achieve. After I complete my next big project or get a raise, I shall buy a new one and gift this to someone in need."

Can you see the difference in thought? Although gratitude journaling sounds simple to a point of seeming ineffective, do not underestimate its power especially when you make it a habit. When you walk down the street looking for things to appreciate in people, the street, passing cars, etc. the effect this will have on your mindset will be tremendous.

Be grateful for everything that adds value to your life. It will teach your subconscious mind to notice the good in everything and because this is part of subconscious reprogramming, the control it will give you over your subconscious will make it your bitch.

In addition, when you get into the habit of gratitude journaling and heaping praise on everything that adds value to your life—or even on random strangers you meet—it will be easier to recognize negative thoughts in time to substitute them with positive ones.

Again, repetition is key. Always remember that nothing worth having comes easy. Practice until noticing negative thoughts and then replacing them with positive ones becomes second nature.

3: Affirmations and Visualization

We have discussed both strategies but only in passing. Here, we shall delve a bit deeper and discuss how to use both strategies effectively to bend your subconscious mind to your will.

First, you already know what affirmations are: statements or sentences meant to influence your mind. Affirmations can be positive or negative both of which manifest through self-talk. When your self-talk is negative, you are reinforcing into your subconscious mind negative programs and thought patterns and therefore, the habits, reactions and behaviors stored in the unconscious mind will be negative, something you do not want. The vice versa is also true.

To use affirmations and visualization to control your subconscious mind and make it do what you want, lace your affirmations with feeling and emotion (we talked about this) and then create a very vivid image of what you want to achieve. For instance, if you want to get your subconscious mind to reflect calm instead of the anxiety of a job interview, you can lace an affirmation such as, "I am calm" with emotions by picturizing yourself in a serene environment that brings you calm. A vivid imagination will lead to better results and more control over the operations of the subconscious mind.

All the three techniques we have discussed here are potent in their own right but are much, much more effective when combined. For instance, as you meditate, since your conscious mind will be more timid, you can plant affirmations and visualizations into your subconscious mind thereby controlling its responses. Likewise, when you meditate on what you are grateful for, the reprogramming happening in the background is indescribable.

Now that you know how to control your subconscious mind and make it your b*tch, because you want to achieve success and experience abundance in all areas of your life, you need to learn how to reprogram the subconscious mind.

By reprogram, we mean replace the default programs in its RAM with better ones. For instance, if you are a pessimist/negative thinker, you can reprogram your subconscious mind so that you make positive thinking the default program.

The next part outlines the steps used to reprogram the subconscious mind.

Rules Of Reprogramming Your Subconscious Mind

As you may have noted, the underlying message presented to you in this guide is that through consistent practice of specific strategies (such as those mentioned in the previous section), you can mold your subconscious mind into whatever you want—what you mold it into will reflect in your physical world and personal life because thoughts are energy. They attract similar energies: negative thoughts attract a negative life while positive thoughts attract a positive, happy life.

If you are like most people, it is likely that you have unknowingly been programming your subconscious—and therefore unconscious mind because the conscious and subconscious minds filter out the memories, beliefs, habits, and perspective stored permanently in the unconscious mind—with the wrong messages aka negative thinking.

If any area of your life is not as you would want it to be, it is because you have been unconsciously reinforcing the wrong thoughts, sentiments, and feelings; these have then directed your subconscious mind towards certain programs.

As implied earlier, conscious awareness of your moment-to-moment thought process is the secret to controlling your subconscious mind and making it your bitch. The last section talked about this at length.

In this section, we are going to discuss the exact steps that will help you deprogram negativity out of your subconscious mind and reprogram it as you see fit (preferable to help you achieve all your goals and heart's desires including wealth, health, and happiness).

How To Reprogram Your Subconscious

Implement the following steps/rules and you will successfully reprogram your subconscious mind:

Step 1: Clarity of aim

Reprogramming your subconscious mind is a lot like creating goals in that both require clarity of purpose or aim. Before you start the process of reprogramming or make changes to the programs in your RAM (subconscious) decide what you want and then define it as clearly as possible because a lack of clarity is how you attract the wrong circumstances. Remember what we said about visualization: the clearer it is, the stronger the emotional attachment, the more bendable your subconscious mind will be.

Clarity of aim also requires that you load one program—the change you want to make—at a time. Reprogramming your mind is very similar to creating new habits—in fact, to reprogram your subconscious mind, habits are the very thing you need to create. For instance, when you form the habit of journaling, using affirmations, meditating, and being mindful, the habits will reprogram and have a clearly visible effect on your physical life.

Know what you want (write the desired outcome on paper), and then if you have several aims, only implement one at a time. Remember repetition is one of the secrets to reprogramming your mind. Focusing on the implementation of more than one aim will only create confusion and discord in your life.

Step/rule 2: Isolate the faulty 'program'

Earlier, we mentioned how the brain is a lot like a computer. Think of what you would do if a computer had a redundant and ineffective program. You would probably uninstall that program and replace it with a more effective one. The mind works similarly.

Whatever circumstance you want to change, you must first realize that your presence in that circumstance comes from a set of programs (habits, beliefs, etc.) you have automatically installed in your subconscious mind.

Before you 'install' a new 'program'—we can also call it habit because repetition leads to the formation of habits—determine the nature of the program you want to uninstall from your subconscious mind. Determine how the program has been keeping you from achieving your goal or the desired outcome. Here, a sincere conversation about why you are where you are right now (the undesired circumstance) will prove very effectual.

Subconscious Mind

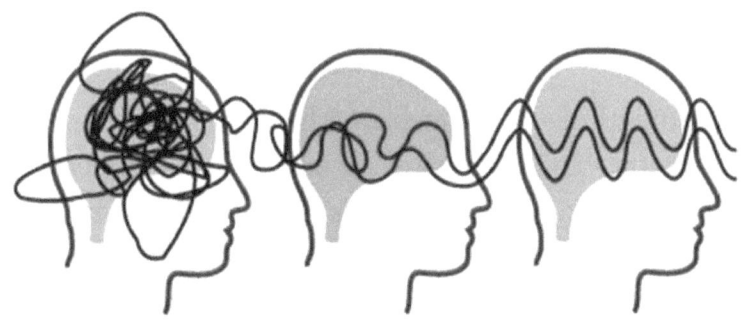

The aim of having a heart-to-heart conversation with yourself is to help you determine and isolate the program (the set of habits and beliefs) that is placing blockades on the path to your goal, wish, or desired circumstance.

Asking yourself, "which program, belief, perspective, or obstacle is keeping me from being Y or achieving X?" will unearth the programs you need to reprogram.

For instance, by asking the above question, a man who is struggling to earn more money may discover that he has a set of limiting beliefs, 'programs,' towards money, or that he has bad habits (also programs formed from repetition) such as a lack of perseverance or procrastination.

By finding the cause, the faulty program, it becomes easier to determine which subjective thoughts, affirmation, and visualization to feed the mind to reprogram habits, beliefs, and programs stored in the subconscious and unconscious mind (the two have a very interrelated relationship).

Step/rule 3: Do it before drifting off to sleep (or first thing in the morning)

Learning something new—such as a habit or reprogramming your subconscious—activates neuronal connectivity, something that activates our alpha brain waves, the waves most predominant in our mind as we day dream. This resource has additional information on brain waves and their effect on the various levels of the mind:

Reprogramming your mind in the moments before you doze off is the most effective time to do it because at this time, the conscious mind relaxes as the body and muscles loosen, and your breathing rate eases and you enter into relaxation mode, alpha brain waves. In these 15 minutes, the pathways between the conscious and subconscious will be open, and it will be easier to implant thoughts, visualizations, affirmations, etc. that help you reprogram your subconscious mind.

Using these three easy to understand steps/rules, you can reprogram any habit, belief, perspective out of your subconscious mind and replace it with whatever program you want depending on your desired outcome.

Bonus! Additional Ways To Communicate With, And Reprogram Your Subconscious Mind

Other than the various methods, steps, and strategies we have discussed, you can also use the following strategies to communicate with your subconscious mind and take control (reprogram it using positive affirmations, visualization, meditation, new habits, or new beliefs).

1: Metaphors

Metaphors are an effective way to communicate with, and program your subconscious mind. To use metaphors for this purpose, implement the following steps:

1. Calming music: In the 15 minutes before you drift off, repetitively play a piece of calming, alpha brainwave music; your conscious mind will get into alpha brain waves, which will make your subconscious mind more receptive and thus easier to program.

2. The message: After getting into a relaxed mode—you can also practice this method during a meditation session—start programming your preferred message into your subconscious (through visualization or affirmation). The fact that the subconscious knows not difference between reality and an imagined reality will work in your favor.

2: The Outcome Technique

This method is an especially effective way to change how the subconscious mind perceives circumstances in your life. Relaxation is also key here. Breath meditation/4-part breathing is an especially effective way to relax on cue and activate alpha brain waves.

To implement the method, follow these steps:

1. The goal or aim: make sure your goal, aim, or desired circumstance is one you truly want.

2. Visualize: Picturize the outcome as clearly as you can in your mind. Visualize yourself being, owning, doing, or having achieved your aim, goal, or desired outcome. See it as clearly as possible.

3. Immerse: Immerse yourself in this visualization. Connect deeply with how it makes you feel. Be the visualization: see, hear, feel, and live it. The clearer it is and the more you feel it, the more effective the programming process will be. Imagine how it will feel to be living in the desired state and then experience everything about it as if it is real—remember, the subconscious does not know it is not real (at least not right now).

These methods are very powerful ways to reprogram your subconscious mind. Keep in mind that repetition is the secret sauce! Practice these strategies and the ones we discussed earlier one at a time until your subconscious mind starts bending to your will and attracting into your life your dreams, aims, aspirations, new habits, perspectives, and above all, healthy programs/habits/beliefs that help you live the life you want.

Conclusion

We have come to the end of the book. Thank you for reading and congratulations for reading until the end.

Let me emphasize that anyone wishing to bring about substantial change in his or her life will at one point or the other have to reprogram the subconscious mind. This guide has shown you the various strategies you can use to communicate with, program, and de-program your subconscious mind and make it your bitch.

Again, repetition is key. Implement each strategy discussed one at a time and remember to implant/change one program/habit at a time.

Now is your turn to take action!

If you found the book valuable, can you recommend it to others? One way to do that is to post a review on Amazon.

Do You Like My Book & Approach To Publishing?

If you like my writing and style and would love the ease of learning literally everything you can get your hands on from Fantonpublishers.com, I'd really need you to do me either of the following favors.

1: First, I'd Love It If You Leave a Review of This Book on Amazon.

2: Check Out My Emotional Mastery Books

Note: This list may not represent all my Keto diet books. You can check the full list by visiting my author page.

Emotional Intelligence: The Mindfulness Guide To Mastering Your Emotions, Getting Ahead And Improving Your Life

Stress: The Psychology of Managing Pressure: Practical Strategies to turn Pressure into Positive Energy (5 Key Stress Techniques for Stress, Anxiety, and Depression Relief)

Failure Is Not The END: It Is An Emotional Gym: Complete Workout Plan On How To Build Your Emotional Muscle And Burning Down Anxiety To Become Emotionally Stronger, More Confident and Less Reactive

Subconscious Mind: Tame, Reprogram & Control Your Subconscious Mind To Transform Your Life

Body Language: Master Body Language: A Practical Guide to Understanding Nonverbal Communication and Improving Your Relationships

Shame and Guilt: Overcoming Shame and Guilt: Step By Step Guide On How to Overcome Shame and Guilt for Good

Anger Management: A Simple Guide on How to Deal with Anger

Get updates when we publish any book that will help you master your emotions: http://bit.ly/2fantonpubpersonaldevl

To get a list of all my other books, please fantonwriters.com, my author central or let me send you the list by requesting them below: http://bit.ly/2fantonpubnewbooks

3: Grab Some Freebies On Your Way Out; Giving Is Receiving, Right?

I gave you a complimentary book at the start of the book. If you are still interested, grab it here.

5 Pillar Life Transformation Checklist: http://bit.ly/2fantonfreebie

PSS: Let Me Also Help You Save Some Money!

If you are a heavy reader, have you considered subscribing to Kindle Unlimited? You can read this and millions of other books for just $9.99 a month)! You can check it out by searching for Kindle Unlimited on Amazon!

www.ingramcontent.com/pod-product-compliance
Lightning Source LLC
Chambersburg PA
CBHW030202100526
44592CB00009B/412